Feast & Be Fit

Feast & Be Fit

OFFICIAL RECIPES
NATIONAL INSTITUTE OF FITNESS

Published by
The National Institute of Fitness
A Division of Franklin Quest Company

Cover photo
The National Institute of Fitness facility is located in
Ivins, Utah, and has as its backdrop the fiery red-rock cliffs
leading to beautiful Snow Canyon. The red rock used in the
cover photo is typical of that surrounding the NIF property.
After you've visited NIF, you'll always remember the beautiful
formations, canyons, and stone monoliths of the area.

Feast & Be Fit   *April 1996 • ©1996 Franklin Quest Company • Salt Lake City, Utah*

Library of Congress Cataloguing-in-Publication Data

Author(s): National Institute of Fitness, a Division
           of Franklin Quest Company
Title: Feast & Be Fit
Sutitle: Official Recipes National Institute of Fitness
Edition: First Edition

Salt Lake City, Utah

Library of Congress ID 96-084979
ISBN 0-9652481-0-0
First Printing: May 1996
160 Pages
$12.95 soft cover

Publication by Publishers Press
a Division of Franklin Quest Company
2200 West Parkway Blvd.
Salt Lake City, UT 84119

Printed in the United States of America
by Publishers Press

Dedication

This recipe book is dedicated to all who strive for improved health through proper nutrition.

"I've been to several spas, and after seeing the NIF facility, staff, education classes, program, cuisine, and beauty services, I think they should charge 2,000 to 3,000 dollars per week, but do not because of their sincere interest in helping others obtain health and fitness."

- Debbie Childs -

"Without a doubt, NIF has the most medically sound program of any spa. I highly endorse it."

- Michael Klaper, M.D. -

"My all-too-brief visit to the National Institute of Fitness proved to be most rewarding. My cholesterol decreased from over 200 to less than 150. I lost weight as well as inches. This is an ideal method to improve eating and exercise habits. The food is most nutritious and the facilities more than adequate for all the exercising your body can take. It is an excellent place to be introduced to behavioral modification."

- Curtis H. Swartz, M.D. San Diego, CA -

Table of Contents

The National Institute of Fitness (NIF)

Our goal is to help you achieve the level of health you desire through excellent nutrition.

Founded in 1974, the National Institute of Fitness is one of the best-known health resorts in the world and is consistently ranked as one of the top ten "spas" in the United States. However, NIF is not really considered a "spa," but rather a retreat where guests can learn to live a healthy lifestyle. NIF activities include hiking and walking, tennis, racquetball, aerobic dance, water exercise, biking, swimming, weight training, as well as cardiovascular conditioning on a variety of treadmills, stair climbers, and cross-training machines. Guests attend lectures on a variety of health subjects. The main focus at NIF is education and exercise. Our other health and appearance services include massages, facials, manicures, and hair styling.

Rooms with maid service and superb meals are part of the NIF experience. Food is plentiful and always available in keeping with the NIF "eat more" philosophy. Weight loss averages about a pound per day for men and about one-half pound per day for women. Other changes experienced by guests often include dramatic drops in blood pressure, blood sugar, and serum cholesterol levels.

The average stay at NIF is about two weeks, but rewards of health and fitness accrue even after one week.

NIF is located at the base of the geologically spectacular Snow Canyon State Park near St. George, Utah. The area features year-round hiking in

wonderfully scenic surroundings. The following national park attractions are located within an hour or two from NIF: Great Basin, Grand Canyon, Zions Canyon, Bryce, Canyonlands, and Arches National Parks. Lake Powell National Recreation Area and Lake Mead National Recreation Area are also nearby.

For more information on the National Institute of Fitness, please call (801) 673-4905 or (888) 444-4230 (toll free), or write:

National Institute of Fitness
202 North Snow Canyon Road
Ivins, Utah 84738

NIF Nutritional Guidelines

Our goal is to help you achieve the level of health you desire through excellent nutrition.

The National Institute of Fitness (NIF) is dedicated to being a positive influence in helping people enjoy healthier, longer, richer, and more fulfilling lives. Those of us in the NIF Food Services Department are excited to make these official recipes available not only to our thousands of guests but also to all who want to maintain a sane, delicious, and healthy diet. We created recipes to provide you with both pleasurable tastes and crucial nutritional benefits.

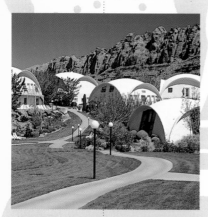

These recipes do not use products high in cholesterol, white flour, or artificial fat. The nutritional standards we use are:

- No meal contains more than 12 percent calories from fat.

- No recipe contains sweetener other than fructose, whole fruit, fruit juice concentrates, pureed fruits, pure maple syrup, or molasses.

- No recipe contains white flour—just whole grain flours such as whole wheat flour, or rolled oats, corn meal, spelt, and brown rice.

We suggest you cut down on fat by teaching your taste buds to appreciate the natural flavors of food without added fat. The successful approach is not to give up the foods you love but to learn to make them the healthy way—without added fat, sugar, and oils—using ingredients that provide the nutrients you need for good health. These recipes use a greater variety of spices and flavorings than traditional recipes.

These official NIF recipes use:

Natural Sweeteners—The delicious sweetness in many of our recipes comes from nutritious ingredients such as whole fruit, fruit-juice concentrate, fructose, pure maple syrup, and molasses. Mashed bananas or applesauce (or pureed fruit) can provide both sweetness and the moist texture that fat provides. You can puree fruit in a blender or food processor, or find pureed fruit with no sugar or fat added in the baby food aisle at the grocery store.

Whole Grains—Our recipes incorporate whole grains in as much as these whole grains contain nutrients in greater quantities because they are less processed and refined than other flours.

You can easily learn to prepare healthy meals.

All ingredients needed for making these NIF-tested recipes are listed in the ingredients section of each recipe. Things will be simplified for you and errors eliminated if you will read each recipe completely before beginning. To achieve the best results, understand and follow each recipe's instructions even more carefully than you would in an ordinary cookbook.

Low-fat cooking is substantially different from traditional cooking. Many baked items will have a different consistency. Instead of cookies being crisp, they will be wonderfully chewy.

You can do more than just enjoy these recipes without guilt. You can feel great by providing your body with foods that will make a positive impact on your health. These recipes are our contribution to improving the way you eat, by showing you how to cut down on fat without giving up the taste and enjoyment of the foods you love.

Nutritional Data

The nutritional analysis for each recipe states:

- Calorie count
- Grams of total fat
- Milligrams of sodium
- Percentage of calories from fat
  (most important of all)

This analysis applies to a single serving, based on the number of servings given for each recipe and the amount of each ingredient listed in the recipe.

For people with special dietary needs, please consult your physician, dietitian, or other health-care provider before changing your food program.

Meal Plan Comparison

FACTOR	AMERICAN NUTRITION	NIF LOW FAT	NIF VEGAN
Calories From Fat	35-40%	10-12%	8-10%
Calories From Protein	15-20%	10-12%	10-12%
Calories From Starch	35-40%	70% or more	70% or more
Animal Product Consumed Per Day	12-16 oz.	2-3 oz.	0 oz.
Cholesterol Consumed Per Day	200-600 mg.	60-80 mg.	0 mg.
Fiber Consumed Per Day	5-6 gr.	50-60 gr.	50-60 gr.
Sodium Consumed Per Day	5000-6000 mg.	Less than 2000 mg.	Less than 2000 mg.
Long-Term Effect on Body Weight	Increase	Decrease	Decrease
Risk of Diseases of Civilization (Heart Disease, Cancer, Stroke, Etc.)	Increase	Decrease	Decrease

Breakfast

A healthy beginning to every day should start with a nutritional breakfast, low in calories and high in energy!

Apple Spice Muffins

Vegan

345 calories

.7 grams fat

249 mg sodium

1.85% calories from fat

2¼ cups whole wheat flour
2 tsp. baking powder
1 tsp. baking soda
½ tsp. allspice
½ tsp. nutmeg
1 tsp. cinnamon

¾ cup apple juice concentrate
¾ cup grated apples
1 tsp. butter extract
½ tblsp. maple extract
¼ cup applesauce
1 tsp. egg replacer

Preheat oven to 375.° Combine all dry ingredients, except the egg replacer, in a mixing bowl and mix thoroughly. Combine all of the wet ingredients. Pour the wet ingredients into the dry ingredients, stirring well. Sprinkle the egg replacer on top and fold in. Spray muffin tins with nonstick food coating. Fill tins ¾ full with batter. Bake for 15-17 minutes. Makes 8 muffins.

Banana grape-nuts® Muffins

Vegan

179 calories

3 grams fat

220 mg sodium

4.2% calories
from fat

2¼ cups whole wheat flour
2   tsp. baking powder
1   tsp. baking soda
⅓   cup fructose
½   cup grape-nuts®
1   tsp. vanilla
1   tsp. banana extract

¼   cup orange juice
     concentrate
1⅓ cups mashed bananas
½   tsp. cinnamon
⅔   tsp. nutmeg
¼   tsp. allspice
¼   cup water
1   tsp. egg replacer

Preheat oven to 375°. Combine all dry ingredients, except the egg replacer, in a mixing bowl and mix thoroughly. Place all remaining ingredients, except the egg replacer, in a blender and puree until smooth. Combine with the dry ingredients. Sprinkle the egg replacer on top and fold in. Spray muffin tins with nonstick food coating. Fill tins ¾ full with batter. Bake for 15-17 minutes. Makes 10 muffins.

Blueberry Muffins

Vegan

197 calories

.73 grams fat

237 mg sodium

3.3% calories from fat

2¼ cups whole wheat flour
2 tsp. baking powder
1 tsp. baking soda
⅓ cup fructose
¼ cup applesauce

1⅓ cups pineapple juice
¾ cup frozen blueberries
1 tsp. vanilla
1 tsp. egg replacer

Preheat oven to 375°. Combine all dry ingredients, except the egg replacer, in a mixing bowl and mix thoroughly. Combine all of the wet ingredients. Pour the wet ingredients into the dry ingredients, stirring well. Sprinkle the egg replacer on top and fold in. Spray muffin tins with nonstick food coating. Fill tins ¾ full with batter. Bake for 15-17 minutes. Makes 8 muffins.

Corn Meal Muffins

Vegan

290 calories

.9 grams fat

281 mg sodium

2.8% calories from fat

1½ cups whole wheat flour
⅔ cup corn meal
2 tsp. baking powder
1 tsp. baking soda
2 tblsp. fructose

½ cup applesauce
½ cup apple juice concentrate
3½ tblsp. water
1 tsp. egg replacer

Preheat oven to 375°. Combine all dry ingredients, except the egg replacer, in a mixing bowl and mix thoroughly. Combine all of the wet ingredients. Pour the wet ingredients into the dry ingredients, stirring well. Sprinkle the egg replacer on top and fold in. Spray muffin tins with nonstick food coating. Fill tins ¾ full with batter. Bake for 15-17 minutes. Makes 7 muffins.

Jelly

Vegan

135 calories

0 grams fat

11 mg sodium

0% calories from fat

1 12-ounce can concentrated juice (apple, orange, grape, etc.)

1 tblsp. cornstarch

1 tblsp. unflavored gelatin

Combine all ingredients in a saucepan. Cook over medium heat, stirring frequently, until mixture comes to a boil. Remove from heat. Pour into containers and refrigerate for 4 hours before serving. Makes 6 servings.

Oat Bran Muffins

Vegan

267 calories

1.2 grams fat

220 mg sodium

3.9% calories from fat

1⅔ cups whole wheat flour
1 cup oat bran
2 tsp. baking powder
1 tsp. baking soda
½ tsp. cinnamon
⅓ cup applesauce

¾ cup apple juice concentrate
1 tsp. maple extract
⅓ tsp. butter extract
⅓ cup water
1 tsp. egg replacer

Preheat oven to 375°. Combine all dry ingredients, except the egg replacer, in a mixing bowl and mix thoroughly. Combine all of the wet ingredients. Pour the wet ingredients into the dry ingredients, stirring well. Sprinkle the egg replacer on top and fold in. Spray muffin tins with nonstick food coating. Fill tins ¾ full with batter. Bake for 15-17 minutes. Makes 9 muffins.

BREAKFAST

Orange Peel Muffins

Vegan

203 calories

.5 grams fat

261 mg sodium

*2.4% calories
from fat*

1⅔ cups whole wheat flour
2 tsp. baking powder
1 tsp. baking soda
1 tsp. orange peel
1 tsp. fructose
¼ cup grape-nuts®
1 tsp. vanilla

¼ cup orange juice concentrate
⅓ cup apple juice concentrate
½ cup applesauce
¼ cup water
1 tsp. egg replacer

Preheat oven to 375˚. Combine all dry ingredients, except the egg replacer, in a mixing bowl and mix thoroughly. Combine all of the wet ingredients. Pour the wet ingredients into the dry ingredients, stirring well. Sprinkle the egg replacer on top and fold in. Spray muffin tins with nonstick food coating. Fill tins ¾ full with batter. Bake for 17-19 minutes. Makes 8 muffins.

Orange Pineapple Muffins

Vegan

189 calories

.65 grams fat

236 mg sodium

*3.1% calories
from fat*

2¼ cups whole wheat flour
2 tsp. baking powder
1 tsp. baking soda
⅓ cup fructose
1 tsp. orange peel
1 tsp. vanilla
¼ cup applesauce

¼ cup pineapple juice
¼ cup orange juice concentrate
½ cup crushed pineapple
½ cup Mandarin orange segments
1 tsp. egg replacer

Preheat oven to 375°. Combine all dry ingredients, except the egg replacer, in a mixing bowl and mix thoroughly. Combine all of the wet ingredients together. Pour the wet ingredients into the dry ingredients, stirring well. Sprinkle the egg replacer on top and fold in. Spray muffin tins with nonstick food coating. Fill tins ¾ full with batter. Bake for 15-17 minutes. Makes 8 muffins.

Pancakes

Vegan

76 calories

.4 grams fat

76 mg sodium

*4.5% calories
from fat*

2 cups whole wheat flour
2 tsp. baking powder
2 tblsp. fructose

¼ tsp. cinnamon
¼ tsp. orange peel
3 cups water (as needed)

Combine all ingredients mixing thoroughly.
Add more water to reach the desired consistency.
Lightly spray the surface of a grill with a nonstick
food coating. Place ½ cup of pancake mix on the
grill. Cook until golden brown, turning once.
Makes 12 servings.

Peach Muffins

Vegan

196 calories

.7 grams fat

240 mg sodium

3% calories from fat

2¼ cups whole wheat flour
2 tsp. baking powder
1 tsp. baking soda
⅓ cup fructose
⅓ cup applesauce
1 tsp. vanilla

1 tsp. cinnamon
⅓ cup water
½ cup peach juice concentrate
¾ cup diced peaches
1 tsp. egg replacer

Preheat oven to 375°. Combine all dry ingredients, except the egg replacer, in a mixing bowl and mix thoroughly. Combine all of the wet ingredients. Pour the wet ingredients into the dry ingredients, stirring well. Sprinkle the egg replacer on top and fold in. Spray muffin tins with nonstick food coating. Fill tins ¾ full with batter. Bake for 17-19 minutes. Makes 8 muffins.

Pumpkin Muffins

Vegan

230 calories

.9 grams fat

213 mg sodium

*3.4% calories
from fat*

2½ cups whole wheat flour

2 tsp. baking powder

1 tsp. baking soda

1 tsp. cinnamon

½ tsp. nutmeg

⅓ cup fructose

½ tsp. pumpkin pie spice

1 tsp. vanilla

⅓ cup apple juice concentrate

1½ cups pumpkin

4 tsp. egg replacer

*Preheat oven to 375.° Combine all dry ingredients,
except the egg replacer, in a mixing bowl and mix
thoroughly. Combine all of the wet ingredients.
Pour the wet ingredients into the dry ingredients,
stirring well. Sprinkle the egg replacer on top and
fold in. Spray muffin tins with nonstick food
coating. Fill tins ¾ full with batter. Bake for 15-
17 minutes. Makes 9 muffins.*

Raspberry Muffins

Vegan

202 calories

.7 grams fat

239 mg sodium

3.1% calories from fat

2¼ cups whole wheat flour
2 tsp. baking powder
1 tsp. baking soda
⅓ cup fructose
1 tsp. vanilla

¼ cup applesauce
¾ cup raspberries, frozen
⅓ cup raspberry juice concentrate
¾ cup pineapple juice
1 tsp. egg replacer

BREAKFAST

Preheat oven to 375°. Combine all dry ingredients, except the egg replacer, in a mixing bowl and mix thoroughly. Combine all of the wet ingredients. Pour the wet ingredients into the dry ingredients, stirring well. Sprinkle the egg replacer on top and fold in. Spray muffin tins with nonstick food coating. Fill tins ¾ full with batter. Bake for 17-19 minutes. Makes 8 muffins.

Lunch

From soup to pizza, pasta to turkey spread, and a whole lot more, these NIF recipes ensure you a healthy midday taste treat!

Beef Barley Soup

Vegan

492 calories

.6 grams fat

391 mg sodium

*1.1% calories
from fat*

5 cups water

½ cup dry pearl barley

⅔ cup grated carrots

⅔ cup diced onions

⅔ cup diced celery

¼ cup beef-flavored
broth base

1 tsp. garlic granules

5 tsp. parsley

1 pinch black pepper

*Place water, barley, carrots, onions, and celery in a
large pot and bring to a boil. Reduce to medium
heat and cook for 40 minutes. Add remaining
ingredients and cook for another 25 minutes.
Makes 3 one-cup servings.*

Black Bean Soup

Vegan

90 calories

.4 grams fat

538 mg sodium

3.9% calories
from fat

1 cup raw black beans
⅔ cup diced carrots
⅓ cup diced onions
⅔ cup diced celery
½ tblsp. garlic powder

½ tsp. cumin
3 tblsp. Bragg™ liquid
   aminos
4 cups water

*Soak black beans overnight in cold water. Drain
and rinse the beans after soaking. Cook the black
beans in water over medium heat for 30 minutes.
Add the garlic powder and cumin and continue
cooking for another 20 minutes. Steam the
vegetables to desired tenderness. Add the
vegetables and the Bragg™ immediately before
serving. Makes 4 one-cup servings.*

LUNCH

Chicken Noodle Soup

Vegan

124 calories

.8 grams fat

213 mg sodium

6.0% calories from fat

8 cups water

8 ounces wide ribbon pasta

1¼ tblsp. parsley

1 cup sliced carrots

½ cup diced celery

½ cup diced onions

⅓ cup chicken-flavored broth base

¹⁄₁₀ tsp. white pepper

Place all the ingredients, except the pasta, into a large pot. Cook for 20 minutes (or longer, depending on desired tenderness for vegetables), over medium heat. Add the pasta and continue cooking for another 10 minutes. Makes 6 one-cup servings.

Chili

Vegan

226 calories

.6 grams fat

241 mg sodium

2.4% calories from fat

1	tblsp. Italian Style Buddy-Burger™
¾	tblsp. water
4	cups water as needed to cook beans
1⅓	cups raw pinto beans
1	cup diced onions
1	tblsp. chili powder
½	tsp. paprika
2	tblsp. minced garlic
½	tsp. cumin

⅒	tsp. pizza seasoning
3	tblsp. beef-flavored broth base
¼	cup diced green peppers
¾	cup diced tomatoes
¾	cup tomato puree
2	tblsp. diced green chilies
½	tsp. maple syrup
¼	tsp. apple cider vinegar

Soak and then rinse beans. After soaking and rinsing the beans, cook over medium heat until tender, or about 1½ hours. Add diced tomatoes, tomato puree, onion, peppers, Buddy-Burger™ (mixed in the ¾ tblsp. water), and chilies. Cook over medium heat for 15 minutes. Add the remaining ingredients, except the vinegar and maple syrup, and continue cooking for another 30 minutes. Add vinegar and maple syrup just before serving. Makes 6 one-cup servings.

Chunky Vegetable Soup

Vegan

310 calories

.2 grams fat

309 mg sodium

.6% calories from fat

2½ cups water
⅓ cup diced tomatoes
⅓ cup tomato puree
4 cups assorted vegetables
1 tsp. basil

1 tsp. oregano
⅛ tsp. black pepper
½ tblsp. minced garlic
⅓ cup beef-flavored broth base

Place the vegetables, diced tomatoes, and water in a large pot and cook over medium heat for 30 minutes. Add the remaining ingredients and continue cooking for another 30 minutes. Makes 6 one-cup servings.

Cucumber Salad

Vegan

30 calories

.1 grams fat

258 mg sodium

2.1% calories
from fat

2 cups sliced cucumbers

½ cup seasoned rice
vinegar

1 tblsp. parsley

¼ cup sliced purple
onions

*Combine all ingredients in a bowl. Allow to
marinate for at least 2 hours before serving. Makes
5 one-half-cup servings.*

LUNCH

Fruit Coleslaw

Vegan

132 calories

.3 grams fat

21 mg sodium

2.3% calories from fat

⅓ head shredded cabbage

14 ounces crushed pineapple

3 tblsp. pineapple juice

⅓ cup raisins

¼ cup fructose

¼ cup dried diced apricots

1 cup diced red apples

3 tblsp. tofu

¼ cup grated carrots

Place fructose, tofu, and pineapple juice in a blender and puree until smooth. Combine all ingredients in a large bowl. Chill before serving. Makes 7 one-half-cup servings.

Garbanzo Bean Spread

Vegan

204 calories

1.3 grams fat

426 mg sodium

5.6% calories from fat

2 cups garbanzo beans

2 tblsp. beef-flavored broth base

1 tblsp. unflavored gelatin

⅔ cup water

½ tsp. garlic

⅓ cup grated carrots

⅓ cup diced celery

⅓ cup diced green onions

¼ cup diced green bell peppers

¼ cup diced red bell peppers

Place the water in a saucepan and bring to a boil. Dissolve the gelatin in the water stirring constantly. Place in a blender along with the garbanzo beans and the broth base. Blend well. Pour into a large mixing bowl, add the vegetables, and mix well. Refrigerate for 4 hours. Use for sandwiches, stuffed tomatoes, and stuffed pitas. Makes 5 one-half-cup servings.

LUNCH

Lentil Soup

Vegan

383 calories

.5 grams fat

244 mg sodium

1.3% calories from fat

1¼ cups raw lentils

¼ cup beef-flavored broth base

⅔ cup diced celery

⅔ cup diced carrots

⅓ cup diced onions

⅓ tsp. garlic

⅛ tsp. white pepper

½ tblsp. parsley

5 cups water

Soak lentils overnight in water. Drain and rinse the lentils after soaking. Cook the lentils over medium heat for 15 minutes. Add all the ingredients and cook for another 10 minutes or until desired tenderness for vegetables. Makes 5 one-cup servings.

Mexican Hominy Soup

Vegan

134 calories

1.2 grams fat

382 mg sodium

7.8% calories from fat

4 cups water

¼ cup chicken-flavored broth base

2¼ cups whole kernel corn

2 tblsp. diced green chilies

¾ tsp. chili powder

⅔ cup diced onions

1½ cups hominy

1 cup sliced mushrooms

Combine all ingredients, except the mushrooms, in a large saucepan and cook over medium heat for 20 minutes. Add mushrooms and cook for another 5 minutes. Makes 6 one-cup servings.

LUNCH

Multi-Bean Soup

Vegan

262 calories

.6 grams fat

394 mg sodium

2.0% calories from fat

1⅓ cups assorted beans

6 cups water

¾ cup diced celery

½ cup diced onions

¾ cup diced carrots

1¾ tsp. hickory smoke

2 tblsp. Bragg™ liquid aminos

5 tsp. beef-flavored broth base

Soak beans overnight in water. Drain and rinse the beans after soaking. Place the beans and the water in a large pot and cook over medium heat for 30 minutes. Add the remaining ingredients, except the hickory smoke, and cook another 30 minutes. Add the hickory smoke immediately before serving. Makes 5 one-cup servings.

Pink Lentil Soup

Vegan

242 calories

.5 grams fat

332 mg sodium

1.7% calories from fat

1¼ cups pink lentils
5 cups water
⅔ cup diced celery
⅔ cup diced carrots
1 cup diced onions
⅛ tsp. dill

⅛ tsp. basil
1 pinch marjoram
1 pinch tarragon
2 tblsp. Bragg™ liquid aminos
2 tblsp. beef-flavored broth base

Soak lentils overnight in water. Drain and rinse the lentils after soaking. Cook the lentils over medium heat for 15 minutes. Add all the ingredients and cook for another 10 minutes or until desired tenderness for vegetables. Makes 5 one-cup servings.

Pizza

Vegan

222 calories

1.4 grams fat

278 mg sodium

5.7% calories from fat

1 cup tomato puree

½ tsp. pizza seasoning

⅛ tsp. beef-flavored broth base

2 cups shredded green bell peppers

2 cups shredded red bell peppers

2 cups diced onions

2 cups sliced mushrooms

8 whole wheat pita pockets

Combine the first three ingredients in a saucepan and simmer for 30 minutes. Spread 2 ounces of sauce over the top of each pita. Top with vegetables. Bake in preheated oven at 375° for 30-35 minutes. Makes 8 servings.

Rotelli Pasta Salad

Vegan

57 calories

.4 grams fat

153 mg sodium

5.8% calories from fat

1 cup whole wheat rotelli pasta

⅔ cup mixed vegetables

⅔ cup steamed broccoli florettes

¼ cup diced red bell pepper

⅔ tsp. basil

1 tsp. oregano

1 pinch black pepper

1 tblsp. Bragg™ liquid aminos

2¾ tblsp. Italian dressing

Cook pasta until tender, according to package directions. Drain pasta and add all remaining ingredients. Mix thoroughly. Makes 6 one-half-cup servings.

Split Pea Soup

Vegan

293 calories

1.0 grams fat

252 mg sodium

3.1% calories from fat

2 cups green split peas, raw

6 cups water

¼ cup chicken-flavored broth base

½ tsp. basil

½ tsp. marjoram

1 tblsp. minced garlic

⅛ tsp. black pepper

½ cup diced celery

½ cup diced carrots

½ cup diced onions

1 tsp. hickory smoke flavor

Rinse split peas before using. Place all ingredients, except for the hickory smoke flavoring, into a saucepan. Simmer until split peas and vegetables are tender, approximately 1 hour. Add the hickory smoke flavoring immediately before serving. Makes 5 one-cup servings.

Tuna Spread

Low Fat

80 calories

.5 grams fat

303 mg sodium

5.5% calories from fat

1   6-ounce can tuna packed in water

3   tblsp. fat-free mayonnaise

2   tblsp. grated carrots

2   tblsp. diced celery

2   tblsp. diced green onions

Drain the water from the canned tuna fish. Add the remaining ingredients, stirring well. Chill for 3 hours before serving. Use for stuffed tomatoes, sandwiches, etc. Makes 3 one-cup servings.

LUNCH

Three Bean Salad

Vegan

137 calories

.5 grams fat

141 mg sodium

3.6% calories from fat

¾ cup kidney beans

¾ cup pinto beans

⅓ cup tomato puree

⅓ cup diced tomatoes

⅓ cup green beans

⅓ cup garbanzo beans

¼ cup sliced purple onions

⅓ cup diced green chilies

2⅔ tblsp. Italian dressing

Drain and rinse all beans. Place all ingredients together in a bowl, mixing carefully. Makes 6 one-half-cup servings.

Tomato Macaroni Soup

Vegan

196 calories

.3 grams fat

229 mg sodium

1.4% calories from fat

1 cup whole wheat elbow noodles

3 cups water

¾ cup tomato puree

¾ cup diced tomatoes

¼ cup chopped onions

¼ cup diced celery

½ cup diced carrots

3 tblsp. chopped green bell peppers

½ cup chopped zucchini

1 tsp. Italian seasoning

½ tsp. garlic powder

1 pinch black pepper

3 tblsp. beef-flavored broth base

Cook the pasta according to package directions. Drain all the water off. Add the noodles to the remaining ingredients. Simmer over medium heat for 20 minutes. Makes 6 one-cup servings.

Tostadas

Vegan

125 calories

.3 grams fat

91 mg sodium

2.2% calories from fat

1¼ cups pinto beans

5 tsp. beef-flavored broth base

½ tblsp. chili powder

⅛ tsp. cumin

1 tsp. minced garlic

2 tblsp. diced green chilies

2 tblsp. minced onions

4 tsp. maza flour

6 whole wheat pita pockets

Soak pinto beans overnight. Drain and rinse. Cook beans in a saucepan over medium heat until tender, approximately 1 hour. Drain the water. Puree the beans in a blender until thick and creamy. Add all remaining ingredients, except for the maza flour, and stir in. Add the maza flour if mixture is too thin. (Beans can be placed in a bowl and mashed with a potato masher instead of in the blender if desired). Place ¾ cup bean mixture on top of whole wheat pita pocket and top with lettuce, tomatoes, mock sour cream, salsa, etc. Makes 6 servings.

Turkey Spread

Low Fat

117 calories

.7 grams fat

324 mg sodium

5.6% calories from fat

6 ounces cooked diced turkey

¼ cup shredded carrots

¼ cup diced celery

¼ cup diced onions

½ cup fat free mayonnaise

⅛ tsp. black pepper

Combine all ingredients in a bowl and mix thoroughly. Chill for 3 hours before serving. Serve over a bed of shredded lettuce. Makes 3 servings.

LUNCH

White Bean Soup

Vegan

165 calories

.6 grams fat

188 mg sodium

3.3% calories from fat

1 cup raw white beans
⅔ cup shredded carrots
⅔ cup chopped celery
⅓ cup diced onions
⅛ tsp. cumin

⅛ tsp. white pepper
1 tsp. minced garlic
3 tblsp. chicken-flavored broth base
1 tblsp. parsley

Soak white beans overnight. Drain and rinse the beans after soaking. Cook the white beans in water over medium heat for 30 minutes. Add all the ingredients, except for the parsley, and continue to cook for another 20 minutes. Add the parsley immediately before serving. Makes 5 one-cup servings.

Dinner

These meals fit a gourmet feast but were created with your nutritional needs and good health in mind!

DINNER

Dinner continued

These meals fit a gourmet feast but were created with your nutritional needs and good health in mind!

Bar-B-Joes *(vegan)*

Vegan

99 calories

.7 grams fat

136 mg sodium

6.6% calories from fat

3 tblsp. plain Buddy-Burger™ Mix

2 tblsp. water

⅓ cup cooked brown rice

1¼ cups tomato puree

⅓ cup diced onions

¾ tsp. mustard

2 tsp. beef-flavored broth base

2 tsp. Bragg™ liquid aminos

1¾ tblsp. fructose

3 tblsp. water

½ tblsp. seasoned rice vinegar

¼ tsp. hickory smoke flavoring

Combine the Buddy-Burger™ mix and the water in a bowl. Set aside while preparing the remaining ingredients. Place all remaining ingredients, except for the vinegar and hickory smoke, in a saucepan. Simmer for 20 minutes. Add the vinegar, hickory smoke, and Buddy-Burger™ mixture immediately before serving. Serve on a whole wheat bun. Makes 6 servings.

DINNER

Bar-B-Joes *(low fat)*

Low Fat

109 calories

.6 grams fat

142 mg sodium

4.9% calories from fat

1⅔ cups tomato puree

½ cup diced onions

1 tsp. mustard

2 tsp. beef-flavored broth base

2 tsp. Bragg™ liquid aminos

2 tsp. seasoned rice vinegar

¼ cup water

3 tblsp. fructose

½ tblsp. hickory smoke flavoring

⅔ pound ground turkey

Cook the ground turkey in a saucepan over medium heat until browned and thoroughly cooked. Drain. Place all ingredients, except for the hickory smoke and vinegar, in a saucepan. Simmer over medium heat for 20 minutes. Add the two remaining ingredients immediately before serving. Serve on a whole wheat bun. Makes 8 servings.

Barbeque Chicken

Low Fat

385 calories

4.6 grams fat

290 mg sodium

10.8% calories
from fat

Sauce:
1 cup tomato puree
¼ cup diced onions
1 tsp. mustard
1 tblsp. chicken-flavored
broth base
1 tblsp. Bragg™ liquid
aminos
1 tblsp. fructose
⅔ cup water
1 tblsp. seasoned rice
vinegar
2 tsp. hickory-smoke
flavoring

1 12-ounce package
whole wheat wide
ribbon noodles
6 3-ounce boneless
skinless chicken
breasts

Combine all sauce ingredients, except for vinegar
and hickory flavoring, in a saucepan and simmer
for 20 minutes. Trim fat from the chicken.
Preheat grill to medium heat. Grill chicken for 5-8
minutes per side or until done. Cook pasta
according to package directions. Immediately
before serving, add vinegar and hickory flavoring to
sauce. Serve chicken and sauce over pasta. Makes
6 servings.

DINNER

Barley Loaf

Vegan

340 calories

1.4 grams fat

239 mg sodium

3.7% calories from fat

1⅓ cups raw barley
1⅓ cups raw millet
4 cups water
⅔ cup grated carrots
⅔ cup diced onions
⅔ cup minced celery
1⅓ cups whole wheat bread crumbs
½ tsp. basil

1 tblsp. parsley
3 tblsp. beef-flavored broth base
⅔ tsp. baking powder
½ tblsp. egg replacer
⅔ tsp. sage
2½ tblsp. whole wheat flour

Preheat oven to 375. Cook the barley for 15 minutes in water over medium heat. Add millet and continue cooking for another 30 minutes. Combine all remaining ingredients in a mixing bowl. Fold in barley and millet. Spray a 5" x 9" baking dish with nonstick spray coating. Place mixture in pan pressing firmly and evenly. Bake for 50-60 minutes. Take out of oven, remove from baking dish, and allow to cool for ½ hour. Cut with serrated knife. Place portions on their side on a baking sheet and bake at 200° for 15 minutes. Make 7 servings.

Brown Rice Pilaf

Vegan

190 calories

1.5 grams fat

170 mg sodium

6.9% calories
from fat

2¼ cups water

3 tblsp. chicken-flavored
   broth base

1⅓ cups raw brown rice

1½ tblsp. parsley

Bring water to a boil. Add all ingredients, except the parsley, to the water, reduce the heat, and simmer for 20 minutes. Add the parsley. Remove from the heat, cover, and allow to sit for 20 minutes before serving. Makes 5 servings.

DINNER

Buddy Burgers

Vegan

224 calories

1.9 grams fat

285 mg sodium

7.6% calories from fat

1½ tblsp. Italian Buddy-Burger™ Mix

1½ tblsp. plain Buddy-Burger™ Mix

¾ cup water

½ cup diced onions

½ cup minced celery

½ tsp. minced garlic

1¼ cups cooked brown rice

¾ cup whole wheat bread crumbs

1 tblsp. beef-flavored broth base

1 tblsp. Bragg™ liquid aminos

½ tblsp. egg replacer

½ tsp. baking powder

¼ cup whole wheat flour

3¼ tsp. water

Preheat grill to medium heat. Combine the Buddy-Burger™ mixes and the water in a bowl. Set aside while preparing the remaining ingredients. Place all remaining ingredients in a bowl and mix thoroughly. Stir in the Buddy-Burger™ mixture. Form mixture into patties. Cook patty 5-6 minutes on each side or until done. Makes 7 servings.

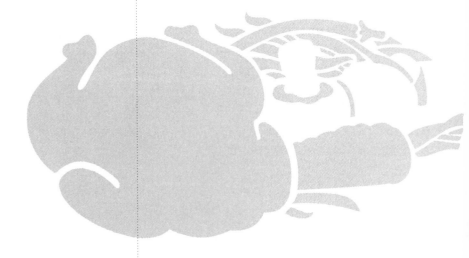

Burritos *(vegan)*

Vegan

342 calories

3.0 grams fat

287 mg sodium

7.8% calories from fat

3 cups raw pinto beans
1 tblsp. minced garlic
1 tsp. cumin
1 cup diced onions
¼ cup diced green chilies

¼ cup beef-flavored broth base
1 tblsp. chili powder
¼ cup tomato puree
10 whole wheat chapatis
¼ cup diced tomatoes

Soak beans in water for 8 hours. Rinse and cook beans for 30 minutes over medium heat or until tender. Place the beans in a bowl and stir in all the remaining ingredients, except for the chapati. Place ¾ cup bean mixture in the middle of the chapati. Serve immediately. Makes 10 servings.

DINNER

Burritos *(low fat)*

Low Fat

326 calories

3.5 grams fat

285 mg sodium

9.6% calories from fat

3 cups raw pinto beans
1 pound ground turkey
2 tblsp. minced garlic
1½ tsp. cumin
1 cup diced onions
½ cup diced green chilies
¼ cup beef-flavored broth base
4 tsp. chili powder
1 cup tomato puree
12 whole wheat chapatis
½ cup diced tomatoes

Soak beans in water for 8 hours. Rinse and cook beans for 30 minutes over medium heat or until tender. Cook the turkey burger in a frying pan until browned. Drain grease from the browned turkey burger. Place the beans and meat into a bowl and stir in all the remaining ingredients, except for the chapatis. Place 1 cup mixture in the middle of the chapati. Serve immediately. Makes 12 servings.

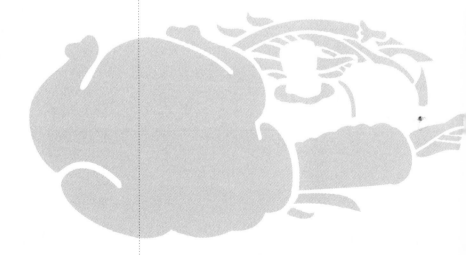

Cabbage Rolls *(vegan)*

Vegan

122 calories

1.9 grams fat

125 mg sodium

13.8% calories from fat

3   tblsp. plain Buddy-Burger™ Mix

3   tblsp. Italian Buddy-Burger™ Mix

1½ cups water

1   cup sausage seitan

1½ tsp. beef-flavored broth base

½   cup cooked brown rice

½   tsp. thyme

½   tsp. basil

½   tsp. sage

8   cabbage leaves

Preheat oven to 325°. Combine the Buddy-Burger™ mixes and the water in a bowl. Set aside while preparing the remaining ingredients. Place all ingredients, except for cabbage leaves, in a large bowl and mix thoroughly. Steam cabbage leaves until tender. Place ½ cup mixture on cabbage leaf and roll. Place cabbage rolls in a 9" x 13" baking dish and add ¼ inch of water. Cover and bake for 45-55 minutes. (Top with mushroom sauce if desired.) Makes 8 servings.

DINNER

Cabbage Rolls *(low fat)*

Low Fat

303 calories

226 grams fat

272 mg sodium

5.5% calories from fat

1 pound ground turkey
½ tsp. rosemary
½ tsp. white pepper
½ tsp. onion powder
1½ tsp. sage
2 cups cooked brown rice
¼ cup diced onions
2 tblsp. beef-flavored broth base
2 tblsp. Bragg™ liquid aminos
8 cabbage leaves

Preheat oven to 325°. Place all ingredients, except for cabbage leaves, in a large bowl and mix thoroughly. Steam cabbage leaves until tender. Place ½ cup mixture on cabbage leaf and roll. Place cabbage rolls in a 9" x 13" baking dish and add ¼ inch of water. Cover and bake for 45-55 minutes. (Top with mushroom sauce if desired.) Makes 8 servings.

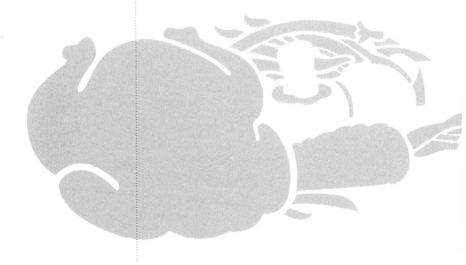

Chicken Cacciatore

Low Fat

368 calories

4.6 grams fat

203 mg sodium

*11.2% calories
from fat*

Sauce:

¾ cup tomato puree

¾ cup diced tomatoes

2 tblsp. chicken-flavored
   broth base

1 tblsp. minced garlic

1 tsp. Italian seasoning

¼ cup water

½ tsp. maple syrup

1 16-ounce package
   whole wheat wide
   ribbon noodles

8 3-ounce boneless
   skinless chicken
   breasts

*Combine all sauce ingredients in a saucepan and
simmer for 20 minutes. Trim fat off the chicken.
Preheat oven to 325°. Place chicken on baking
sheet and cook until done. Cook pasta according to
package directions. Serve chicken and sauce over
pasta. Makes 8 servings.*

DINNER

Chinese Stirfry

Vegan

335 calories

3.6 grams fat

513 gm sodium

9.7% calories from fat

Marinade:

½ cup Bragg™ liquid aminos

⅓ cup maple syrup

2½ tsp. minced garlic

½ tsp. black pepper

1 block tofu, 14-ounce, cut into ¼ inch pieces

⅓ cup mirin

2 tblsp. grated ginger

¼ tsp. allspice

½ tsp. coriander

2 cups julienned shiitake mushrooms

1½ cups julienned carrots

1 cup julienned red bell peppers

2 cups julienned onions

1½ cups julienned daikon radish

2 cups julienned bok choy

1½ cups sugar snap peas

1 tblsp. cornstarch

1 cup cold water

1 8.8-ounce package udon noodles

Combine all marinade ingredients in a mixing bowl. Place all vegetables, except for the sugar snap peas, in with the marinade sauce and allow to marinate for 2-3 hours. Remove all of the vegetables and place in a saucepan. Stir fry over medium heat for 10-15 minutes or until tender, using ½ of the marinade liquid. Add more marinade sauce, if needed, so the vegetables do not burn. Add the sugar snap peas. Dissolve the cornstarch in the cold water. Thicken as needed with cornstarch mixture. Cook udon noodles according to package directions. Serve over udon noodles. Makes 6 servings.

Cous Cous

Vegan

68 calories

.1 grams fat

50 mg sodium

1.3% calories from fat

1¾ cups water

1   tblsp. chicken-flavored broth base

2   cups raw cous cous

Place water in a saucepan and bring to a boil. Stir in broth base and cous cous. Remove from heat and continue stirring for 1 minute. Makes 6 servings.

DINNER

Curry Vegetables

Vegan

119 calories

.4 grams fat

303 mg sodium

2.7% calories from fat

1 cup julienned onions

2 tblsp. apple juice concentrate

3 cups raw chopped red potatoes

2 cups julienned baby carrots

1 cup julienned green bell peppers

1 cup wedged tomatoes

½ cup peeled and chopped eggplant

½ cup water

1 cup frozen peas

1 tblsp. minced garlic

1½ tsp. grated ginger

1½ tsp. curry powder

1 tblsp. maple syrup

½ tsp. raw apple cider vinegar

¼ cup Bragg™ liquid aminos

Saute onions in apple juice concentrate over medium heat until translucent. Steam potatoes and carrots in another pan for 6 minutes or to desired tenderness. Add potatoes and carrots to onions and continue cooking over medium heat for 15 minutes. At any time during cooking add water as needed. Stir in peppers, tomatoes, and egg plant and continue cooking for 10 more minutes. Add remaining ingredients and remove from stove. Do not over stir vegetables. Serve over golden rice. Makes 10 servings.

Enchiladas

Vegan

335 calories

1.3 grams fat

272 mg sodium

*3.4 calories
from fat*

1¼ cups raw pinto beans
3 cups water
¼ cup diced onions
1 tblsp. chili powder
⅛ tsp. cumin
1 tsp. minced garlic
2 tblsp. diced green chilies
1 tblsp. maza flour
2 tblsp. beef-flavored broth base

6 corn tortillas

Sauce:
1¾ cups tomato puree
1½ cups water
1 tsp. chili powder
⅛ tsp. cumin
½ cup diced onions
2 tblsp. beef-flavored broth base

Soak beans in water for 8 hours. Rinse and cook beans for 30 minutes over medium heat or until tender. Place beans in a blender and puree. Add water if needed. Preheat oven to 325˚. Combine all sauce ingredients in a saucepan and simmer for 20 minutes. Place beans and all remaining ingredients, except for tortillas, in a bowl and mix thoroughly. Dip tortilla in the sauce. Place ½ cup bean mixture on tortilla and roll. Spray a 9" x 13" baking dish with nonstick spray coating. Place tortillas in baking dish. Pour ½ of remaining sauce on top of tortillas and bake for 30-40 minutes. Serve with remaining sauce. Makes 6 servings.

DINNER

German Meatballs

Low Fat

292 calories

2.3 grams fat

385 mg sodium

*7.0% calories
from fat*

1	pound ground turkey
1	cup cooked brown rice
1	cup raw oats
1	cup diced onions
3	tblsp. parsley
3	tblsp. Bragg™ liquid aminos

3	tblsp. beef-flavored broth base
1	tsp. lemon peel
1	tsp. rosemary
1	tsp. lemon juice
¼	tsp. paprika
½	tsp. ground nutmeg

Preheat oven to 375°. Place all ingredients in a mixing bowl and mix thoroughly. Take ½ cup mixture and form into balls. Place on baking sheet. Bake uncovered for 1 hour, turning once. Makes 8 servings.

Golden Rice

Vegan

70 calories

.6 grams fat

3 mg sodium

7.6% calories from fat

3 cups water

1 cup raw brown rice

¾ tsp. anise seeds

¾ tsp. turmeric

Place water in a saucepan and bring to a boil. Add all remaining ingredients, cover and simmer for 15 minutes. Remove from heat, cover, and allow to sit for 20 minutes before serving. Makes 10 servings.

DINNER

Grilled Italian Chicken

Low Fat

332 calories

4.3 grams fat

282 mg sodium

*11.7% calories
from fat*

5 tblsp. orange juice concentrate

5 tblsp. Italian dressing

6 3-ounce boneless skinless chicken breasts

Trim fat from the chicken. Combine juice and dressing. Pour over chicken and allow to marinate for 3-4 hours. Preheat grill to medium heat. Grill chicken for 5-7 minutes per side or until done. Makes 6 servings.

Rice:

2¼ cups water

3 tblsp. chicken-flavored broth base

1⅓ cups raw brown rice

1½ tblsp. parsley

Bring water to a boil. Add all ingredients, except the parsley, to the water, reduce the heat, and simmer for 20 minutes. Add the parsley. Remove from the heat, cover, and allow to sit for 20 minutes before serving. Makes 5 servings.

Mashed Potatoes

Vegan

125 calories

.1 grams fat

174 mg sodium

1.0% calories from fat

7 cups peeled cooked potatoes

¼ cup soy milk

2 tblsp. Bragg™ liquid aminos

⅓ tsp. butter extract

¼ tblsp. onion powder

½ tblsp. parsley

1 tsp. minced garlic

Place all ingredients in a mixing bowl. Mix on high with hand mixer for 3 minutes. For a more moist consistency add more soy milk. Makes 8 servings.

DINNER

Meatloaf

Low Fat

251 calories

2.1 grams fat

268 mg sodium

7.7% calories from fat

1 pound ground turkey
1 cup cooked brown rice
1 cup raw oats
⅓ tsp. sage
½ tsp. oregano
½ tsp. black pepper
1½ tsp. minced garlic
¼ cup diced onion
2 tblsp. Bragg™ liquid aminos
2 tblsp. beef-flavored broth base

Preheat oven to 350°. Combine all ingredients in a bowl and mix thoroughly. Spray a 5" x 9" baking dish with nonstick spray coating. Press mixture evenly in pan and cover. Bake for 40-50 minutes. Top with mushroom sauce if desired. Makes 8 servings.

Mexican Crepes *(vegan)*

Vegan

168 calories

2.6 grams fat

257 mg sodium

14.2% calories
from fat

Sauce:

¼	cup cornstarch	2	cups water
¼	cup cold water	2	tblsp. diced onions
2	tblsp. chicken-flavored broth base	¼	cup diced mushrooms
¼	tsp. chili powder	1	tblsp. diced green chilies

Dissolve cornstarch in cold water and set aside. Combine all remaining ingredients in a saucepan and bring to a boil. Thicken as needed with cornstarch mixture. Set aside.

Filling:

1½	cups diced chicken seitan	2	tblsp. diced green chilies
2	tblsp. diced onions	¾	cup diced mushrooms
		6	whole wheat chapatis

Place all of the above ingredients, except for the chapatis, in a mixing bowl and combine thoroughly.

Preheat oven to 350°. Place ¼ cup sauce and ½ cup filling on the center of each chapati and roll. Spray a 9" x 13" baking dish with nonstick food coating. Place rolled chapatis on dish. Pour ½ cup sauce over the top of the chapatis. Cover and bake for 15-20 minutes. Makes 6 servings.

DINNER

Mexican Crepes *(low fat)*

Low Fat

244 calories

4.6 grams fat

266 mg sodium

17% calories from fat

Sauce:

¼	cup cornstarch	2	cups water
¼	cup cold water	2	tblsp. diced onions
2	tblsp. chicken-flavored broth base	¼	cup diced mushrooms
¼	tsp. chili powder	1	tblsp. diced green chilies

Dissolve cornstarch in cold water and set aside. Combine all remaining ingredients in a saucepan and bring to a boil. Thicken as needed with cornstarch mixture. Set aside.

Filling:

1½	cups cooked diced chicken	2	tblsp. diced green chilies
2	tblsp. diced onions	¾	cup diced mushrooms
		6	whole wheat chapatis

Place all of the above ingredients, except for the chapatis, in a mixing bowl and combine thoroughly.

Preheat oven to 350°. Place ¼ cup sauce and ½ cup filling on the center of each chapati and roll. Spray a 9" x 13" baking dish with nonstick food coating. Place rolled chapatis in dish. Pour ½ cup sauce over the top of the chapatis. Cover and bake for 15-20 minutes. Makes 6 servings.

Moroccan Vegetables

Vegan

154 calories

.9 grams fat

298 mg sodium

5.1% calories from fat

1½ cups julienned onions

⅓ cup chopped red bell peppers

1½ tsp. minced garlic

1 cup diced tomatoes

1¼ cups diced celery

1½ cups sliced carrots

1 cup diced turnips

1½ tblsp. apple juice concentrate

⅓ cup chopped dried apricots

1 cup cooked garbanzo beans

¼ cup raisins

1½ tblsp. water

⅓ tsp. fennel seed powder

⅛ tsp. turmeric powder

¾ tsp. paprika

1 pinch cayenne pepper

⅓ tsp. cinnamon

¾ tsp. cumin

Saute onions in apple juice concentrate for 8-10 minutes or until translucent. Steam the carrots, turnips, and celery until tender. Add steamed vegetables to the onions and continue to cook for 10 minutes. Combine the water with all dry seasonings. Add all remaining ingredients and seasoned water to vegetable mixture and cook for 5 minutes. Serve over cooked cous cous. Makes 6 servings.

DINNER

Mushroom Sauce

Vegan

73 calories

.02 grams fat

66 mg sodium

.2% calories from fat

2 tblsp. cornstarch
2 tblsp. cold water
1 cup water
2 tblsp. beef-flavored broth base

2 tblsp. diced onions
¾ tblsp. parsley
⅓ cup sliced mushrooms

Dissolve cornstarch in cold water and set aside. Combine all remaining ingredients in a saucepan and bring to a boil. Thicken as needed with cornstarch mixture. Makes 8 servings.

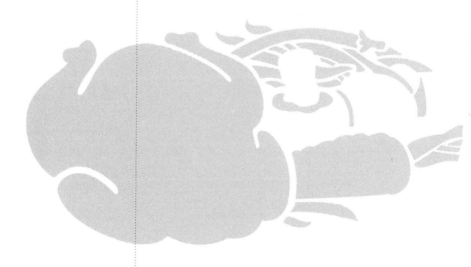

Oriental Dumplings

Vegan

90 calories

1.2 grams fat

320 mg sodium

12.0% calories from fat

Marinade:

¾ cup tofu

1 tsp. baking powder

5½ tsp. Bragg™ liquid aminos

½ tblsp. egg replacer

½ cup julienned carrots

½ cup diced green onions

½ cup julienned yellow squash

½ cup julienned green bell pepper

½ cup julienned red bell pepper

⅓ cup chopped water chestnuts

½ cup sliced mushrooms

½ cup julienned celery

½ cup sugar snap peas

½ cup mung bean sprouts

2 tsp. mustard powder

2 tsp. Bragg™ liquid aminos

1 tsp. minced garlic

1 tsp. grated ginger

⅔ cup spelt flour

Combine all of the marinade ingredients in a blender and puree until smooth. Marinate the remaining ingredients in the marinade for 2-3 hours. Preheat oven to 400°. Spray cookie baking sheet with nonstick spray coating. Form ½ cup mixture into a patty and place on baking sheet. Cook for 20 minutes. Reduce heat to 375° and continue to cook for 15 minutes. Top with pineapple glaze sauce (page 71). Makes 7 servings.

DINNER

Pineapple Glaze Sauce

Vegan

28 calories

0 grams fat

26 mg sodium

0% calories from fat

2 tblsp. cornstarch

2 tblsp. cold water

1 12-ounce can pineapple chunks

1 tblsp. pineapple juice

1½ tblsp. mirin

2 tsp. seasoned rice vinegar

1 tsp. grated ginger

½ tsp. minced garlic

Dissolve cornstarch in cold water. Set aside. Place all remaining ingredients in a saucepan and bring to a boil. Thicken as needed with cornstarch mixture. Makes 7 servings.

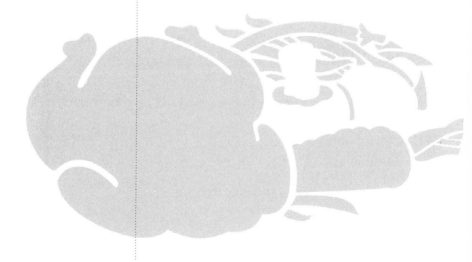

Polenta

Vegan

99 calories

.6 grams fat

251 gm sodium

5.1% calories from fat

6 cups water
2 cups polenta
1 tsp. pizza seasoning

¼ cup Bragg™ liquid aminos
2 tblsp. minced garlic

Place water in a saucepan and bring to a boil. Place all remaining ingredients in the water and simmer for 15-20 minutes or until thick, stirring constantly. Pour mixture into a 9" x 13" baking dish. Chill for 3-4 hours before serving. Preheat oven to 400°. Remove chilled mixture from pan and cut into 12 pieces. Place pieces on a baking sheet and heat in oven for 30 minutes. Top with black beans and red pepper salsa. Makes 12 servings.

Black Beans:

2¾ cups raw black beans
8 cups water
1 tblsp. cumin
½ cup diced onions
1 tblsp. chili powder

1 tblsp. minced garlic
¼ tblsp. Bragg™ liquid aminos
¼ cup maple syrup
¼ tsp. cayenne pepper

Soak the beans in water for at least 8 hours. Drain the water off and cook the beans in fresh water. Bring the water to a boil, reduce heat, and simmer for 30 minutes. Add all remaining ingredients and simmer for 10 more minutes. Serve over the top of the polenta. Makes 12 servings.

DINNER

Potato Salad

Vegan

91 calories

.7 grams fat

178 mg sodium

7.4% calories from fat

Sauce:

1 cup tofu

2¼ tblsp. Italian dressing

1 pinch black pepper

2¼ tblsp. soy milk

½ tblsp. mustard

2¼ tblsp. Bragg™ liquid aminos

5 cups diced boiled potatoes

⅓ cup diced red bell pepper

⅓ cup diced green bell pepper

⅓ cup diced celery

½ cup diced onions

Place all of the sauce ingredients in a blender and puree until smooth. Place all other ingredients in a mixing bowl. Pour the blended sauce over the top. Stir until all ingredients are mixed together thoroughly. Chill for three hours before serving. Makes 10 servings.

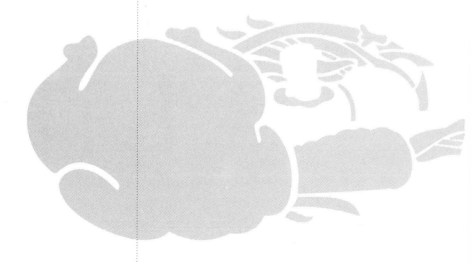

Red Pepper Salsa

Vegan

14 calories

.1 grams fat

4 mg sodium

7.0% calories from fat

2 cups chopped red bell peppers

2 cups diced green onions

1 cup chopped cilantro

1 tblsp. minced garlic

2 tblsp. lemon juice

2 cups diced cucumbers

Place all of the ingredients in a mixing bowl and mix thoroughly. Chill for several hours before serving. Serve with polenta and black beans. Makes 12 servings.

DINNER

Red Bell Pepper Sauce

Vegan

37 calories

.1 grams fat

127 mg sodium

*1.5% calories
from fat*

1 tblsp. cornstarch

1 tblsp. cold water

2 cups chopped red bell peppers

¼ cup diced onions

½ tsp. minced garlic

1 tblsp. apple juice concentrate

1 tblsp. Bragg™ liquid aminos

1½ cups water

⅔ cup wine or raspberry vinegar

*Dissolve cornstarch in cold water and set aside.
Clean the red bell peppers. Steam and puree in a
blender. Combine all remaining ingredients in a
saucepan and bring to a boil. Thicken as needed
with cornstarch mixture. Makes 8 servings.*

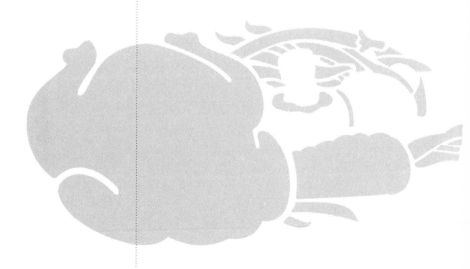

Rice Pilaf

Vegan

200 calories

1.3 grams fat

48 mg sodium

5.9% calories from fat

1⅓ cups raw brown rice

1¾ cups water

½ cup diced onions

¼ cup chopped red bell peppers

½ cup sliced mushrooms

⅔ tsp. chili powder

1 pinch black pepper

2¾ tblsp. beef-flavored broth base

2 tsp. parsley

Place water in a saucepan and bring to a boil. Add all remaining ingredients, except for parsley, cover and simmer for 15 minutes. Remove from heat and allow to sit for 20 minutes before serving. Stir in parsley immediately before serving. Makes 6 servings.

DINNER

Sage Dressing

Vegan

132 calories

.1 grams fat

360 mg sodium

*.5% calories
from fat*

8 cups whole wheat bread (broken into pieces)
1 cup diced celery
1 cup diced onions
¾ tblsp. poultry seasoning

1 tblsp. egg replacer
½ tblsp. sage
3 tblsp. chicken-flavored broth base
1¼ cups water
2¼ tsp. butter extract

Preheat oven to 350°. Dissolve the broth base in the water, add the butter extract, and set aside. Place all remaining ingredients in a mixing bowl and toss together, then add liquid mixture and mix thoroughly. (Add more water to moisten if desired.) Spray a 5" x 9" baking dish with nonstick spray coating. Press mixture into pan evenly. Bake uncovered for 40-50 minutes. Makes 10 servings.

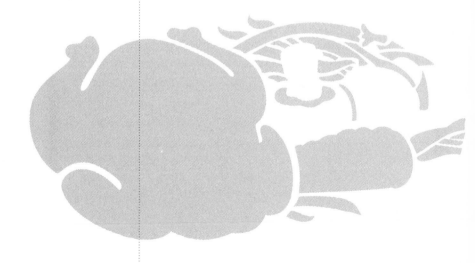

Sausage Patties

Low Fat

250 calories

2.2 grams fat

267 mg sodium

8.1% calories from fat

½ pound ground turkey
½ cup cooked brown rice
½ cup raw oats
1 pinch black pepper
½ tsp. sage

½ tblsp. ground coriander
1 tblsp. beef-flavored broth base
1 tblsp. Bragg™ liquid aminos

Preheat grill to medium heat. Place all ingredients in a mixing bowl and mix thoroughly. Form mixture into patties. Cook patty 5-6 minutes on each side or until done. Makes 4 servings.

DINNER

Spaghetti

Vegan

372 calories

1.5 grams fat

276 mg sodium

3.7% calories from fat

1⅔ cups diced tomatoes

1⅔ cups tomato puree

1¼ tblsp. Italian seasoning

1 tblsp. minced garlic

¼ cup beef-flavored broth base

⅔ cup sliced mushrooms

½ cup water

1 16-ounce package whole wheat spaghetti noodles

Place all ingredients, except for the pasta, in a saucepan and bring to a boil. Simmer for 30 minutes. Cook pasta according to package directions. Serve sauce over cooked pasta. Makes 8 servings.

Spelt Pasta Salad

Vegan

189 calories

1.5 grams fat

124 mg sodium

7.3% calories from fat

⅓ cup chopped zucchini

¼ cup chopped yellow squash

¼ cup chopped green bell peppers

¼ cup chopped red bell peppers

⅔ cup sliced cherry tomatoes

⅔ cup sliced mushrooms

⅓ cup diced green onions

Sauce:

1 tsp. apple cider vinegar

1 tblsp. Bragg™ liquid aminos

1 tblsp. lemon juice

1 tsp. fructose

2 tsp. lemon pepper

1½ tsp. minced garlic

⅓ tsp. oregano

2 tsp. basil

⅓ cup arrowroot mixture

1 8-ounce package Rotini spelt pasta

Place all salad ingredients in a mixing bowl and toss well. Place all sauce ingredients in a blender and puree. Cook the pasta according to package directions. Combine salad ingredients, sauce, and pasta immediately before serving. Makes 5 servings.

DINNER

Stuffed Acorn Squash

Vegan

286 calories

1.0 grams fat

244 mg sodium

3.1% calories from fat

1½ cups raw wild rice

3 cups water

1 tblsp. beef-flavored broth base

¾ cup sliced mushrooms

2 tblsp. Bragg™ liquid aminos

3 tblsp. diced zucchini

½ cup chopped red bell pepper

1 cup water

½ cup diced onions

1 tsp. oregano

2 tsp. basil

½ tsp. minced garlic

½ cup water

¾ cup raw brown rice

1 tblsp. beef-flavored broth base

4 acorn squash

¾ cup corn bread crumbs

Place the wild rice and water in a saucepan and bring to a boil. Reduce heat and simmer for 15 minutes. Stir in the broth base, remove from heat, cover, and allow to sit for 20 minutes. Place the Bragg™ and water in a saucepan with all vegetables. Saute over medium heat for 15 minutes. Add all other ingredients, except for the acorn squash, and simmer for 10-15 minutes or until all water is absorbed. Preheat oven to 375.° Stir in the wild rice mixture. Cut acorn squash in half lengthwise, clean out seeds, and steam until tender. Fill each acorn squash with ¾ cup rice mixture and place on a 9" x 13" baking dish. Bake covered for 45-50 minutes. Uncover and bake for another 10 minutes. Top with mushroom sauce. Makes 8 servings.

Stuffed Green Peppers

Low Fat

266 calories

2.3 grams fat

269 mg sodium

7.8% calories from fat

1	pound ground turkey	2	tsp. rosemary
1	cup raw oats	1	tblsp. minced garlic
1	cup cooked brown rice	½	cup diced onions
½	tsp. white pepper	2	tblsp. Bragg™ liquid aminos
2	tblsp. beef-flavored broth base		
2	tsp. sage	2	tsp. thyme
		4	green bell peppers

Preheat oven to 375°. Cut peppers in half lengthwise. Discard the insides and clean the shells thoroughly. Place all ingredients in a mixing bowl and mix thoroughly. Place ½ cup mixture in each pepper half. Place filled pepper in a 9" x 13" baking dish and cover with ¼ inch of water. Cover and bake for 45-55 minutes. (Top with mushroom sauce if desired). Makes 8 servings.

DINNER

Stuffed Red Peppers

Vegan

188 calories

.8 grams fat

163 mg sodium

3.9% calories from fat

1 cup raw short grain brown rice

2½ cups water

⅓ cup raw wild rice

⅔ cup water

2 tblsp. beef-flavored broth base

¼ cup raisins

2 tblsp. mirin

⅔ cup diced green onions

¼ cup chopped chestnuts

⅔ cup shredded celery

2 tblsp. chopped mint leaves

⅔ tsp. five spice powder

1 tblsp. Bragg™ liquid aminos

4 red bell peppers

Preheat oven to 400°. Cook the brown rice in the water for 45 minutes. Cook the wild rice in the water for 1 hour. Add the broth base to the wild rice and cook for 30 more minutes. Cut peppers in half lengthwise. Discard the insides and clean the shells thoroughly. Place all ingredients in a mixing bowl and mix thoroughly. Place ½ cup mixture in each pepper half. Place filled pepper in a 9" x 13" baking dish and cover with ¼ inch of water. Cover and bake for 45-55 minutes. Top with red bell pepper sauce if desired. Makes 8 servings.

Stuffed Zucchini *(vegan)*

Vegan

203 calories

1.2 grams fat

558 mg sodium

5.5% calories from fat

3	zucchini
⅓	cup raw millet
⅔	cup water
2	cups cooked garbanzo beans
¼	cup diced green chilies
⅓	cup diced onions
2	tblsp. beef-flavored broth base
½	tsp. chili powder

⅛	tsp. cumin
½	tsp. minced garlic
4	tsp. egg replacer
½	tsp. baking powder
⅔	cup whole wheat bread crumbs
⅓	cup maza flour
⅓	cup minced zucchini
1	tblsp. Bragg™ liquid aminos

Preheat oven to 375? Cut each zucchini in half lengthwise, clean out seeds, and set aside. Place water and millet in saucepan and bring to a boil, reduce heat, and simmer for 10 minutes. Place garbanzo beans in a blender and puree, adding water if needed. Combine all ingredients in a mixing bowl and mix thoroughly. Place ½ cup mixture into each zucchini half. Place into a 9" x 13" baking dish. Place ¼ cup water into bottom of baking dish. Cover and bake for 40-50 minutes or until zucchini is cooked. Top with Mexican sauce. Makes 6 servings.

DINNER

Stuffed Zucchini *(low fat)*

Low Fat

231 calories

2.2 grams fat

212 mg sodium

8.6% calories from fat

1	pound ground turkey
1	cup cooked brown rice
1	cup raw oats
¼	cup diced onions
¼	cup diced green chilies
¼	tsp. cumin powder
½	tsp. chili powder
4	tsp. beef-flavored broth base
4	tsp. Bragg™ liquid aminos
4	zucchini

Preheat oven to 350°. Cut zucchini in half lengthwise, clean out seeds, and set aside. Place all remaining ingredients in a mixing bowl and mix thoroughly. Place ½ cup meat mixture into each zucchini half. Place zucchini into a 9" x 13" baking dish. Place ¼ inch of water on the bottom of baking dish. Cover and bake for 45-55 minutes. Top with Mexican sauce. Makes 8 servings.

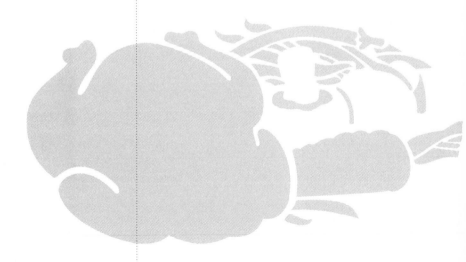

Sweet and Sour Chicken

Low Fat

404 calories

4.5 grams fat

327 mg sodium

*10.1% calories
from fat*

Sauce:

2	tsp. cornstarch	6	ounces pineapple chunks
2	tsp. cold water		
½	cup pineapple juice	6	tblsp. sliced green bell pepper
2	tsp. vinegar		
2	tsp. chicken-flavored broth base	6	tblsp. red bell peppers
2	tsp. fructose	5	3-ounce boneless skinless chicken breasts

Dissolve the cornstarch in the cold water. Set aside. Combine all remaining sauce ingredients in a saucepan and bring to a boil. Thicken as needed with cornstarch mixture. Trim fat from the chicken. Preheat oven to 325°. Place chicken on baking sheet and cook until done. Serve sauce over brown rice pilaf and chicken. Makes 5 servings.

Rice:

2¼ cups water	1⅓ cups raw brown rice
3 tblsp. chicken-flavored broth base	1½ tblsp. parsley

Bring water to a boil. Add all ingredients, except the parsley, to the water, reduce the heat, and simmer for 20 minutes. Add the parsley. Remove from the heat, cover, and allow to sit for 20 minutes before serving. Makes 5 servings.

DINNER

Turkey Burger

Low Fat

210 calories

2.1 grams fat

267 mg sodium

*7.7% calories
from fat*

1   pound ground turkey
1   cup cooked brown rice
1   cup raw oats
¼   cup diced onions

2   tblsp. beef-flavored broth base
2   tblsp. Bragg™ liquid aminos
⅔   tsp. Kitchen Bouquet™

Preheat grill to medium heat. Place all ingredients in a mixing bowl and mix thoroughly. Form mixture into patties. Cook patty 5-6 minutes on each side or until done. Makes 8 servings.

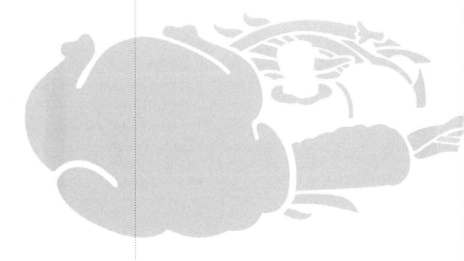

Desserts

The following recipes add a wonderful exclamation point to your nutritious meal—low in fat and calories, high in goodness and great taste!

Apple Cobbler

Vegan

474 calories

.5 grams fat

231 mg sodium

.89% calories from fat

4 cups whole wheat flour
4 tsp. baking powder
2 tsp. baking soda
½ cup fructose
1 tblsp. cinnamon
1 tblsp. vanilla

1 cup applesauce
1½ cups apple juice concentrate
¾ cup water
4 tsp. egg replacer

Preheat oven to 375°. Combine all dry ingredients, except for the egg replacer, in a mixing bowl and mix thoroughly. Combine all of the remaining ingredients and mix thoroughly. Pour the wet ingredients into the dry ingredients, stirring well. Sprinkle the egg replacer on top and fold in. Spray a 9" x 13" baking dish with nonstick spray coating. Bake for 30-35 minutes. Makes 20 servings.

Topping:

⅓ cup cornstarch
⅓ cup cold water
2 tsp. cinnamon

3½ cups apple juice concentrate
2 cups sliced apples
1 cup diced apples

Dissolve cornstarch in water and set aside. Combine all remaining ingredients in a saucepan and bring to a boil. Thicken as needed with cornstarch mixture. Remove from heat and pour over pieces of cake. Makes 20 servings.

Apple Rum Cake

Vegan

176 calories

.8 grams fat

108 mg sodium

4.0% calories from fat

2¼ cups whole wheat flour
2 cups rolled oats
2¼ tsp. baking powder
1 tsp. baking soda
2 tsp. cinnamon
½ tsp. allspice
2¼ tsp. maple syrup

1½ cups sliced apples
⅔ cup applesauce
½ cup raisins
¾ cup apple juice concentrate
2 tsp. rum extract
1 tsp. butter extract
2 tsp. egg replacer

Preheat oven to 375°. Combine all dry ingredients, except for the egg replacer, in a mixing bowl and mix thoroughly. Combine all of the wet ingredients in a separate mixing bowl and mix thoroughly. Pour the wet ingredients into the dry ingredients, stirring well. Sprinkle the egg replacer on top and fold in. Spray a 9" x 13" baking dish with nonstick spray coating. Bake for 30-35 minutes. Makes 20 servings.

Banana Cake

Vegan

144 calories

.9 grams fat

72 mg sodium

5.9% calories from fat

2 cups whole wheat flour

2 cups raw oats

2 tsp. baking powder

½ tsp. baking soda

¼ tsp. maple syrup

¼ tsp. cinnamon

¼ tsp. allspice

½ cup soy milk

⅔ cup orange juice concentrate

1 tsp. banana extract

3 cups mashed bananas

1 tsp. vanilla

1 cup raisins

2 tsp. egg replacer

Preheat oven to 375°. Combine all dry ingredients, except for the egg replacer, in a mixing bowl and mix thoroughly. Combine all of the wet ingredients in a separate mixing bowl and mix thoroughly. Pour the wet ingredients into the dry ingredients, stirring well. Sprinkle the egg replacer on top and fold in. Spray a 9" x 13" baking dish with nonstick spray coating. Bake for 30-35 minutes. Makes 20 servings.

Blueberry Cheesecake

Vegan

205 calories

1.7 grams fat

88 mg sodium

7.4% calories from fat

1 cup grape-nuts®
½ cup water
¼ cup unflavored gelatin
1 14-ounce block tofu

½ cup fat free soy milk
½ cup fructose
1 tblsp. vanilla
1 tblsp. lemon juice

Place grape-nuts® evenly in the bottom of a 9" pie dish. Set aside. Bring water to a boil in a saucepan. Add gelatin and dissolve thoroughly, stirring for 2 minutes. Place gelatin mixture and all remaining ingredients in a blender and puree until smooth. Slowly pour mixture over the top of the grape-nuts® crust. Allow to set up for 3-4 hours in the refrigerator. Serve with two ounces of fruit sauce. Makes 10 servings.

Topping:

¼ cup cornstarch
¼ cup cold water
⅓ cup raspberry juice concentrate
¼ cup cherry juice concentrate

⅓ cup grape juice concentrate
⅔ cup water
2¾ cups frozen blueberries

Dissolve cornstarch in cold water. Set aside. Place all remaining ingredients, except for blueberries, in a saucepan and bring to a boil. Thicken as needed with cornstarch mixture. Stir in the blueberries. Allow to chill for 30 minutes before serving on top of cheesecake. Makes 10 servings.

Blueberry Pineapple Cake

Vegan

137 calories

.5 grams fat

189 mg sodium

3.6% calories from fat

4 cups whole wheat flour
4 tsp. baking powder
2 tsp. baking soda
½ cup fructose
2½ tsp. vanilla
½ cup applesauce
½ cup pineapple juice
1 20-ounce can crushed pineapple
2 cups frozen blueberries
4 tsp. egg replacer

Preheat oven to 375°. Combine all dry ingredients, except for the egg replacer, in a mixing bowl and mix thoroughly. Combine all of the wet ingredients, except for the blueberries, in a separate mixing bowl and mix thoroughly. Pour the wet ingredients into the dry ingredients, stirring well. Sprinkle the egg replacer on top and fold in. Stir in the blueberries slightly so as not to break them up. Spray a 9" x 13" baking dish with nonstick spray coating. Bake for 30-35 minutes. Makes 20 servings.

Bread Pudding

Vegan

354 calories

.04 grams fat

190 mg sodium

.1% calories from fat

10 cups whole wheat bread pieces

1¾ cups water

½ cup raisins

⅓ cup maple syrup

1 tblsp. vanilla

1 tblsp. cinnamon

1 tsp. butter extract

1 tblsp. egg replacer

Preheat oven to 375°. Combine all ingredients, except for the egg replacer, in a mixing bowl and mix thoroughly. Sprinkle the egg replacer on top and fold in. Spray a 9" x 13" baking dish with nonstick spray coating. Bake for 20-25 minutes. Makes 20 servings.

Topping:

½ cup cornstarch

½ cup cold water

2½ cups apple juice concentrate

2¼ cups water

½ tsp. rum extract

½ tsp. brandy extract

Dissolve the cornstarch in the cold water. Set aside. Place all remaining ingredients in a saucepan and bring to a boil. Thicken as needed with cornstarch mixture. Makes 20 servings.

Carob Cake

Vegan

272 calories

.7 grams fat

104 mg sodium

2.3% calories from fat

4½ cups whole wheat flour
4 tsp. baking powder
¾ cup carob powder
2 tblsp. pero® powder
1 cup water

½ cup maple syrup
2 tsp. vanilla
1 cup apple juice concentrate
1 cup applesauce
3½ tsp. egg replacer

Preheat oven to 375.° Combine all dry ingredients, except for the egg replacer, in a mixing bowl and mix thoroughly. Combine all of the wet ingredients in a separate mixing bowl and mix thoroughly. Pour the wet ingredients into the dry ingredients, stirring well. Sprinkle the egg replacer on top and fold in. Spray a 9" x 13" baking dish with nonstick spray coating. Bake for 30-35 minutes. Chill cake before serving. Makes 20 servings.

Carrot Pineapple Cookies

Vegan

76 calories

.2 grams fat

39 mg sodium

3.0% calories from fat

1⅓ cups whole wheat flour

½ tsp. baking powder

¼ tsp. baking soda

⅔ tsp. cinnamon

¼ cup fructose

⅓ tsp. ginger

⅓ cup applesauce

1 8-ounce can crushed pineapple

⅓ cup raisins

⅓ tsp. vanilla

3 cups grated carrots

1 tsp. egg replacer

Preheat oven to 375°. Combine all dry ingredients, except for the egg replacer, in a mixing bowl and mix thoroughly. Combine all of the wet ingredients in a separate mixing bowl and mix thoroughly. Pour the wet ingredients into the dry ingredients, stirring well. Sprinkle the egg replacer on top and fold in. Spray cookie sheet pan with nonstick spray coating. Bake for 8-12 minutes or until done. Makes 16 servings.

Cherry Cobbler

Vegan

208 calories

.5 grams fat

203 mg sodium

2.2% calories from fat

4 cups whole wheat flour
4 tsp. baking powder
2 tsp. baking soda
½ cup fructose
1 tblsp. cinnamon
1 tblsp. vanilla

1 cup applesauce
½ cup cherry juice concentrate
¾ cup pineapple juice
4 tsp. egg replacer

Preheat oven to 375°. Combine all dry ingredients, except for the egg replacer, in a mixing bowl and mix thoroughly. Combine all of the remaining ingredients and mix thoroughly. Pour the wet ingredients into the dry ingredients, stirring well. Sprinkle the egg replacer on top and fold in. Spray a 9" x 13" baking dish with nonstick spray coating. Bake for 30-35 minutes. Makes 20 servings.

Topping:

¼ cup cornstarch
¼ cup cold water
2 cups cherry juice concentrate

2 cups frozen cherries
¾ cup water

Dissolve cornstarch in water and set aside. Combine all remaining ingredients in a saucepan and bring to a boil. Thicken as needed with cornstarch mixture. Remove from heat and pour over pieces of cake. Makes 20 servings.

Fruit Gelatin

Vegan

75 calories

.1 grams fat

3 mg sodium

1.2% calories from fat

1¾ cups water
1   tblsp. unflavored gelatin
6   tblsp. orange flavored gelatin
6   tblsp. lemon flavored gelatin
1¼ cups fruit

Bring water to a boil in a saucepan. Add all gelatins and dissolve thoroughly, stirring for 2 minutes. Pour the gelatin liquid into a 9" x 13" baking dish. Place the fruit in the pan with the liquid. Chill in refrigerator for 3-4 hours before serving. Makes 9 servings.

DESSERT

Ginger Bread

Vegan

182 calories

.7 grams fat

121 mg sodium

3.3% calories from fat

5 cups whole wheat flour
5 tsp. baking powder
1 tblsp. cinnamon
2 tblsp. ginger
½ tsp. allspice

½ cup applesauce
1½ cups maple syrup
2 cups soy milk
2 tsp. egg replacer

Preheat oven to 375°. Combine all dry ingredients, except for the egg replacer, in a mixing bowl and mix thoroughly. Combine all of the remaining ingredients and mix thoroughly. Pour the wet ingredients into the dry ingredients, stirring well. Sprinkle the egg replacer on top and fold in. Spray a 9" x 13" baking dish with nonstick spray coating. Bake for 30-35 minutes. Makes 20 servings.

Lemon Pudding

Vegan

137 calories

1.5 grams fat

10.68 mg sodium

10% calories from fat

¾ cup lemon flavored gelatin

1 tblsp. unflavored gelatin

½ cup water

1 14-ounce block tofu

½ cup fat free soy milk

⅔ cup fructose

1 tblsp. lemon juice concentrate

1 tsp. lemon extract

1 cup ice

Bring water to a boil in a saucepan. Add both gelatins and dissolve thoroughly, stirring for two minutes. Set aside. Place all remaining ingredients in a blender and blend until smooth. Pour in the gelatin mixture and continue to blend thoroughly. Chill in refrigerator for 20-30 minutes before serving. Makes 10 servings.

DESSERT

Orange Chiffon Pie

Vegan

151 calories

1.5 grams fat

78 mg sodium

*8.7% calories
from fat*

1   cup grape-nuts®
½   cup water
¼   cup unflavored gelatin
1   14-ounce block tofu

1   cup orange juice
    concentrate
½   cup fat free soy milk
⅓   cup fructose
1   tblsp. vanilla

*Place grape-nuts® in the bottom of a pie dish. Set
aside. Bring water to a boil in a saucepan. Add
gelatin and dissolve thoroughly, stirring for two
minutes. Place gelatin mixture and all remaining
ingredients in a blender and puree until smooth.
Slowly pour mixture over the top of the grape-nuts®
crust. Allow to set up for 3-4 hours in the
refrigerator. Makes 10 servings.*

Peach Cobbler

Vegan

225 calories

.5 grams fat

208 mg sodium

2.0% calories
from fat

4 cups whole wheat flour
4 tsp. baking powder
2 tsp. baking soda
½ cup fructose
1 tblsp. cinnamon
1 tblsp. vanilla

1 cup applesauce
1½ cups peach juice concentrate
¾ cup water
4 tsp. egg replacer

Preheat oven to 375°. Combine all dry ingredients, except for the egg replacer, in a mixing bowl and mix thoroughly. Combine all of the remaining ingredients and mix thoroughly. Pour the wet ingredients into the dry ingredients, stirring well. Sprinkle the egg replacer on top and fold in. Spray a 9" x 13" baking dish with nonstick spray coating. Bake for 30-35 minutes. Makes 20 servings.

Topping:

⅓ cup cornstarch
⅓ cup cold water
2 cups peach juice concentrate

2 cups frozen sliced peaches
½ tsp. allspice
2 tsp. cinnamon

Dissolve cornstarch in water and set aside. Combine all remaining ingredients in a saucepan and bring to a boil. Thicken as needed with cornstarch mixture. Remove from heat and pour over pieces of cake. Makes 20 servings.

DESSERT

Pineapple Cake

Vegan

208 calories

.4 grams fat

196 mg sodium

1.9% calories from fat

4	cups whole wheat flour
4	tsp. baking powder
2	tsp. baking soda
½	cup fructose
2½	tsp. vanilla

⅔	cup applesauce
1	20-ounce can crushed pineapple
1½	cups pineapple juice
4	tsp. egg replacer

Preheat oven to 375°. Combine all dry ingredients, except for the egg replacer, in a mixing bowl and mix thoroughly. Combine all of the remaining ingredients and mix thoroughly. Pour the wet ingredients into the dry ingredients, stirring well. Sprinkle the egg replacer on top and fold in. Spray a 9" x 13" baking dish with nonstick spray coating. Bake for 30-35 minutes. Makes 20 servings.

Topping:

⅓	cup cornstarch
⅓	cup cold water
2	20-ounce cans crushed pineapple

½	cup fructose
½	cup pineapple juice

Dissolve the cornstarch in the cold water. Set aside. Place all remaining ingredients in a saucepan and bring to a boil. Thicken as needed with cornstarch mixture. Makes 20 servings.

Pumpkin Pie

Vegan

142 calories

1.1 grams fat

82 mg sodium

6.6% calories
from fat

1	cup grape-nuts®
¼	cup water
2	tblsp. unflavored gelatin
½	14-ounce block tofu
1⅓	cups fat free soy milk
⅔	cup fructose
1	tblsp. vanilla
2	tsp. pumpkin pie spice
2	cups canned pumpkin

Place grape-nuts® in the bottom of a pie dish. Set aside. Bring water to a boil in a saucepan. Add gelatin and dissolve thoroughly, stirring for two minutes. Place gelatin mixture and all remaining ingredients in a blender and puree until smooth. Slowly pour mixture over the top of the grape-nuts® crust. Allow to set up for 3-4 hours in the refrigerator. Makes 10 servings.

DESSERT

Raspberry Cheesecake

Vegan

204 calories

1.6 grams fat

91 mg sodium

*7.0% calories
from fat*

1 cup grape-nuts®

½ cup water

¼ cup unflavored gelatin

1 14-ounce block tofu

½ cup fat-free soy milk

½ cup fructose

1 tblsp. vanilla

1 tblsp. lemon juice

Place grape-nuts® in the bottom of a pie dish. Set aside. Bring water to a boil in a saucepan. Add gelatin and dissolve thoroughly, stirring for two minutes. Place gelatin mixture and all remaining ingredients in a blender and puree until smooth. Slowly pour mixture over the top of the grape-nuts® crust. Allow to set up for 3-4 hours in the refrigerator. Serve with 2 ounces of fruit sauce. Makes 10 servings.

Topping:

¼ cup cornstarch

¼ cup cold water

1 cup raspberry juice concentrate

1½ cups water

2¾ cups frozen raspberries

Dissolve cornstarch in cold water. Set aside. Place all remaining ingredients, except for raspberries in a saucepan and bring to a boil. Thicken as needed with cornstarch mixture. Stir in the raspberries. Allow to chill for 30 minutes before serving on top of cheesecake. Makes 10 servings.

Raspberry Cookies

Vegan

30 calories

.1 grams fat

51 mg sodium

3.0% calories
from fat

¾ cup whole wheat flour
½ tblsp. baking powder
¼ tsp. baking soda
3 tblsp. fructose
2 tblsp. applesauce

1 tsp. raspberry extract
¼ cup pineapple juice
¼ cup frozen raspberries
1 tsp. egg replacer

Preheat oven to 350°. Combine all dry ingredients, except for the egg replacer, in a mixing bowl and mix thoroughly. Combine all of the remaining ingredients, except for the raspberries and the egg replacer and mix thoroughly. Pour the wet ingredients into the dry ingredients, stirring well. Sprinkle the egg replacer on top and fold in. Stir in the raspberries slightly. Spray cookie baking sheet with nonstick spray coating. Bake for 8-12 minutes. Makes 18 servings.

Raspberry Pudding

Vegan

124 calories

1.5 grams fat

11 mg sodium

11% calories from fat

¾ cup raspberry flavored gelatin

1 tblsp. unflavored gelatin

½ cup water

1 14-ounce block tofu

½ cup fat-free soy milk

½ cup fructose

1 tblsp. raspberry juice concentrate

1 tsp. raspberry extract

1 cup ice

Bring water to a boil in a saucepan. Add both gelatins and dissolve thoroughly, stirring for two minutes. Set aside. Place all remaining ingredients in a blender and blend until smooth. Pour in the gelatin mixture and continue to blend thoroughly. Chill in refrigerator for 20-30 minutes before serving. Makes 10 servings.

Strawberry Cake

Vegan

470 calories

.4 grams fat

221 mg sodium

.9% calories
from fat

4 cups whole wheat flour
4 tsp. baking powder
2 tsp. baking soda
½ cup fructose
1 tblsp. almond extract
1 tblsp. vanilla

1 cup applesauce
1½ cups cherry juice concentrate
⅔ cup pineapple juice
4 tsp. egg replacer

Preheat oven to 375°. Combine all dry ingredients, except for the egg replacer, in a mixing bowl and mix thoroughly. Combine all of the remaining ingredients, except for the egg replacer and mix thoroughly. Pour the wet ingredients into the dry ingredients, stirring well. Sprinkle the egg replacer on top and fold in. Spray a 9" x 13" baking dish with nonstick spray coating. Bake for 30-35 minutes. Makes 20 servings.

Topping:

¼ cup cornstarch
¼ cup cold water
3 cups apple juice concentrate

¾ cup strawberry flavored gelatin

Dissolve the cornstarch in the cold water. Set aside. Place all remaining ingredients in a saucepan and bring to a boil. Thicken as needed with cornstarch mixture. Makes 20 servings.

Zucchini Cookies

Vegan

110 calories

.3 grams fat

107 mg sodium

2.7% calories from fat

1½ cups whole wheat flour
1 tblsp. baking powder
¼ cup raw oats
⅓ tsp. baking soda
⅔ tsp. cinnamon
½ tblsp. lemon peel
⅓ tsp. nutmeg
⅓ cup fructose

⅓ cup apple juice concentrate
⅓ tsp. maple extract
⅓ cup applesauce
¼ cup raisins
⅓ tsp. vanilla
⅓ tsp. butter extract
⅓ cup grated zucchini
½ tblsp. egg replacer

Preheat oven to 375°. Combine all dry ingredients, except for the egg replacer, in a mixing bowl and mix thoroughly. Combine all the remaining ingredients, and mix thoroughly. Pour the wet ingredients into the dry ingredients, stirring well. Sprinkle the egg replacer on top and fold in. Spray a cookie baking sheet with nonstick spray coating. Bake for 8-12 minutes or until golden brown. Makes 16 servings.

Dressings/Miscellaneous

These special
NIF dressing
recipes will
add zest to
your salads
and nutrition
to your life!

Arrowroot Mixture

Vegan

46 calories

.01 grams fat

7 mg sodium

.2% calories
from fat

1 cup arrowroot powder

1 cup cold water

½ gallon water

Dissolve the arrowroot in the cold water. Set aside. Place the water in a saucepan and bring to a boil. Slowly add the arrowroot mixture to the boiling water, stirring constantly. Allow to chill before using in any recipe. Use as a substitute for oil in salad dressings. Makes 10 servings.

Chili Spice Dressing

Vegan

62 calories

.2 grams fat

185 mg sodium

2.6% calories from fat

½ cup lemon juice concentrate

½ cup apple juice concentrate

2 cups arrowroot mixture

1 tblsp. chili powder

2 tblsp. paprika

2 tsp. minced garlic

⅓ cup Bragg™ liquid aminos

Place all ingredients in a blender and puree until smooth. Chill before serving. Makes 15 servings.

Creamy Cucumber Dressing

Vegan

57 calories

.7 grams fat

78 mg sodium

*11.1% calories
from fat*

1	14-ounce block tofu
4	tsp. minced garlic
1	cup lemon juice
½	cup apple juice concentrate

½	cup fructose
2	tblsp. dill
4	cups arrowroot mixture
¼	cup Bragg™ liquid aminos

*Place all ingredients in a blender and puree until
smooth. Pour into a container and stir in the
following:*

4   cups shredded
    cucumbers

Chill before serving. Makes 20 servings.

Dijon Style Mustard Dressing

Vegan

39 calories

.6 grams fat

435 mg sodium

13.0% calories from fat

¼ cup dijon style mustard

1 tsp. minced garlic

¾ cup seasoned rice vinegar

1½ cups arrowroot mixture

2 tblsp. fresh parsley

Place all ingredients in a blender and puree until smooth. Chill before serving. Makes 15 servings.

Fresh Salsa

Vegan

14 calories

.1 grams fat

55 mg sodium

7.0% calories from fat

6   each serrano peppers

1½ tsp. minced garlic

3   cups chopped tomatoes

2   cups diced tomatoes

1   cup diced onion

1   cup chopped cilantro

1   cup diced green bell peppers

Place the first three ingredients in a blender and puree until smooth. Pour into a mixing bowl and stir in the remaining ingredients. Chill before serving. Makes 20 servings.

Garden Dressing

Vegan

21 calories

.1 grams fat

184 mg sodium

*5.5% calories
from fat*

1½ cups chopped green bell pepper

1 cup chopped red bell pepper

⅔ cup chopped celery

1 tblsp. fresh parsley

1 tsp. minced garlic

⅓ cup chopped purple onion

1⅔ cups chopped tomatoes

1 tblsp. fresh basil

¼ cup seasoned rice vinegar

2 tblsp. Bragg™ liquid aminos

Place all ingredients in a blender and blend briefly so as not to puree. Chill before serving. Makes 13 servings.

Italian Dressing

Vegan

26 calories

.1 grams fat

190 mg sodium

2.5% calories from fat

⅔ cup apple cider vinegar

2 tsp. minced garlic

1 tsp. black pepper

¼ cup lemon juice

¼ cup Bragg™ liquid aminos

1 tblsp. oregano

1 tblsp. basil

2 cups arrowroot mixture

3 tblsp. fructose

Place all ingredients in a blender and puree until smooth. Chill before serving. Makes 14 servings.

Orange Ginger Dill Dressing

Vegan

43 calories

1 grams fat

194 mg sodium

1.0% calories from fat

⅓ cup orange juice concentrate

½ tsp. minced garlic

½ cup seasoned rice vinegar

1 tblsp. grated ginger

2 tsp. dill

¾ cup arrowroot mixture

Place all ingredients in a blender and puree until smooth. Chill before serving. Makes 10 servings.

Parsley Garlic Dressing

Vegan

16 calories

.1 grams fat

37 mg sodium

5.5% calories from fat

3 cups chopped fresh parsley

3 tsp. minced garlic

½ cup apple cider vinegar

2 tsp. Bragg™ liquid aminos

2 cups arrowroot mixture

1 tblsp. fructose

Place all ingredients in a blender and puree until smooth. Chill before serving. Makes 15 servings.

Salsa

Vegan

26 calories

.02 grams fat

139 mg sodium

.7% calories from fat

1¼ cups tomato puree

1¼ cups diced tomatoes

⅓ cup diced green chilies

¼ cup Italian dressing

Mix all ingredients in a mixing bowl and combine thoroughly. Chill before serving. Makes 12 servings.

Seitan

Vegan

105 calories

.4 grams fat

201 mg sodium

*3.9% calories
from fat*

12 cups water
⅛ cup maple syrup

1¼ cups gluten flour
¾ tblsp. garlic powder
¾ tblsp. onion powder
½ tblsp. basil
1 tblsp. chicken-flavored
broth base

1¼ cups water
⅛ cup Bragg™ liquid
aminos

*Place the water and the maple syrup in a large
saucepan and bring to a boil. Mix the next group
of ingredients in a mixing bowl. Combine the
water and the Bragg™ and pour into the dry
ingredients. This will form into a wet dough.
Knead the dough for five minutes trying to get the
air bubbles out. Tear into lemon-sized pieces and
place in the boiling water. Boil for approximately
45 minutes. Remove, cool, and drain in a
colander. Can be frozen.*

Variation:
*For sausage flavored seitan, make the following
changes to the above recipe: Substitute beef-
flavored broth base for the chicken-flavored broth
base.*

Add:
2 tblsp. thyme
2 tblsp. sage
2 tblsp. fennel

Makes 5 servings.

Spicy Italian Dressing

Vegan

40 calories

.1 grams fat

105 mg sodium

1.6 calories from fat

½ cup lemon juice concentrate

½ cup apple juice concentrate

2 cups arrowroot mixture

⅓ cup Bragg™ liquid aminos

¼ cup pizza seasoning

½ cup chopped onions

1½ tsp. minced garlic

2 cups chopped red bell peppers

2 cups chopped green bell peppers

2 cups chopped tomatoes

Place all ingredients in a blender and puree until smooth. Chill before serving. Makes 35 servings.

Sweet Bell Pepper Dressing

Vegan

50 calories

.1 grams fat

110 mg sodium

1.1% calories
from fat

½ cup lemon juice
concentrate

½ cup apple juice
concentrate

2 cups arrowroot
mixture

¼ cup Bragg™ liquid
aminos

3 cups chopped red bell
peppers

1 tsp. black pepper

1 tsp. minced garlic

2 tblsp. basil

*Place all ingredients in a blender and puree until
smooth. Chill before serving. Makes 25 servings.*

Carob Powder: A chocolate substitute without caffeine, made from carob beans. When a recipe calls for cocoa, use an equal amount of carob powder instead.

Cous Cous: Partially cooked cracked wheat. Cous Cous is more refined than bulgur wheat.

Egg Replacer: This is a non-dairy product made from potato starch and tapioca flour with no added preservatives, artificial flavors, or colors. Use one ½ teaspoon per egg. Fold into dry ingredients immediately before baking.

Fructose: Use in place of white granulated sugar. For every one cup of sugar use ⅔ cup fructose. Fructose is a natural sugar that comes from fruit. Use in place of brown sugar by adding maple extract.

Kamut: Ancient food of the Egyptians once thought extinct. Non-hybrid relative of wheat but more nutritious.

Mirin: Mirin is a sweet cooking wine made from whole grain rice. It tenderizes and enhances sautes and sauces by imparting natural sweeteners.

Polenta: Course ground whole corn used in Mediterranean dishes.

Soy Milk: A non-dairy, nonfat product made from soy beans. Use in place of milk in a recipe.

Spelt: Non-hybrid grain similar to wheat. Many wheat-sensitive individuals tolerate it very well because of its great solubility. It can be substituted for wheat in any recipe. Spelt comes in flour, pasta, and bread forms.

Tofu: Pressed soy bean curd. Use in main dishes, desserts, dips, creamy salad dressings, baked goods, etc. Tofu takes on the flavor of any spice or seasoning you blend it with.

Vanilla: 100% pure vanilla extract from a vanilla bean. No alcohol, chemicals, or colors added.

Measurements

A pinch	⅛ Teaspoon or less
3 Teaspoons	1 Tablespoon
4 Tablespoons	¼ Cup
8 Tablespoons	½ Cup
12 Tablespoons	¾ Cup
16 Tablespoons	1 Cup
2 Cups	1 Pint
4 Cups	1 Quart
16 Ounces	1 Pound
1 Fluid Ounce	2 Tablespoons
8 Fluid Ounces	1 Cup
32 Fluid Ounces	1 Quart

Substitutions

Cornstarch	1 tblsp. =	2 Tblsps. Flour
Fresh Herbs	1 tblsp. =	1 Tsp. Dried Herbs
Fresh Onion	1 Small =	1 Tblsp. Minced
Dry Mustard	1 tblsp. =	1 Tblsp. Prepared Mustard
Tomato Juice	1 Cup =	½ Cup Tomato Sauce + ½ Cup Water
Bananas	3 Medium =	1 Cup Mashed Bananas
Sugar	1 Cup =	⅔ Cup Fructose
Sugar	1 Cup =	1½ Cups Fruit Juice Concentrate (Unsweetened)
Sugar	1 Cup =	½ Cup Molasses
Sugar	1 Cup =	¾ Cup Maple Syrup
Oil	1 Cup =	1 - 2 Cups Applesauce (Unsweetened)

Cooking Guide

Cooking Beans

Beans 1 Cup Dry	Amount of Water	Cooking Time	Yield
Black Beans	3 Cups	1½ Hours	2¼ Cups
Garbanzo Beans	4 Cups	3 Hours	2½ Cups
Kidney Beans	3 Cups	1½ Hours	2 Cups
Lentils	3 Cups	1 Hour	2¼ Cups
Navy Beans	3 Cups	2 Hours	2 Cups
Pinto Beans	3 Cups	2½ Hours	2¼ Cups
Split Peas	3 Cups	1 Hour	2½ Cups

Allow beans to soak for at least eight hours (not necessary for lentils or split peas). Discard soaking water, rinse beans, and begin cooking beans in fresh water. Allow to simmer for the specified amount of time.

Cooking Grains

Grain 1 Cup Dry	Amount of Water	Cooking Time	Yield
Barley	3 Cups	1¼ Cups	3½ Cups
Brown Rice	2 Cups	1 Hour	3 Cups
Buckwheat	2 Cups	15 Minutes	2½ Cups
Cous Cous	1½ Cups	10 Minutes	1½ Cups
Millet	3 Cups	45 Minutes	3½ Cups
Polenta	4 Cups	15 Minutes	4 Cups
Whole Wheat	3 Cups	2 Hours	2½ Cups

Most grains are cooked in the following manner: Bring water to a boil and then add the grain. Allow water to return to a boil, then reduce to a simmer, cover, and cook the specified amount of time. For cous cous, add the grain to the boiling water, cover, and remove from heat and let stand. For polenta, stir frequently during cooking time to avoid lumps.

Cooking Terms

Au Jus: Served in its own juices.

Blanch: To immerse in rapidly boiling water and allow to cool.

Degrease: To remove fat from the surface of stews, gravies, soups, or stock. Usually cooled in the refrigerator so fat hardens and is easily removed.

Dredge: To coat lightly with flour, cornmeal, etc.

Entree: The main course.

Julienne: To cut vegetables or fruits into match-sized slivers.

Marinate: To allow food to stand in a liquid to tenderize or to add flavor.

Mince: To chop or cut food into very small pieces.

Parboil: To boil until partially cooked, to blanch. Usually this process is followed by final cooking in a seasoned glaze.

Pare: To remove the outermost skin of a fruit or vegetable.

Poach: To cook very gently in hot liquid kept just below the boiling point.

Puree:	To mash foods until perfectly smooth by hand, by rubbing through a sieve or food mill, or by whirling in a blender or food processor.
Refresh:	To run cool water over food that has been parboiled to stop the cooking process quickly.
Scald:	To heat just below the boiling point when tiny bubbles appear at the edge of the saucepan.
Simmer:	To cook in liquid just below the boiling point. The surface of the liquid should be barely moving, broken from time to time by slowly rising bubbles.
Steep:	To let food stand in hot liquid to extract or to enhance flavor, like tea in hot water.
Toss:	To combine ingredients with a lifting motion.
Whip:	To beat rapidly to incorporate air and produce expansion.

Notes

Notes

_____

_____

_____

_____

_____

_____

_____

_____

_____

_____

_____

_____

_____

_____

_____

_____

_____

Notes

Notes

Notes

Notes

_____

_____

_____

_____

_____

_____

_____

_____

_____

_____

_____

_____

_____

_____

_____

_____

_____

Notes

Notes